DOVER · THRIFT · EDITIONS

Chicago Poems

CARL SANDBURG

DOVER PUBLICATIONS, INC.
New York

DOVER THRIFT EDITIONS

GENERAL EDITOR: STANLEY APPELBAUM
EDITOR OF THIS VOLUME: PHILIP SMITH

Bibliographical Note

This Dover edition, first published in 1994, contains the unabridged text of *Chicago Poems*, first published by Henry Holt and Company, New York, in 1916. A new introductory Note and the alphabetical lists of titles and first lines have been specially prepared for the present edition.

International Standard Book Number: 0-486-28057-8

Manufactured in the United States of America
Dover Publications, Inc., 31 East 2nd Street, Mineola, N.Y. 11501

Note

CARL SANDBURG was born in Galesburg, Illinois on January 6, 1878. He began working at the age of 11 and held a variety of jobs — barbershop porter, milk truck driver, brickyard worker and wheat harvester. Sandburg enlisted in the 6th Illinois Infantry at the outbreak of the Spanish-American War in 1898. In 1913 he moved to Chicago where he became one of a group of writers responsible for the "Chicago Renaissance" of arts and letters.

Sandburg's first success as a poet came with the publication of "Chicago" in *Poetry* magazine in 1914; this poem and others were published in book form in 1916 as *Chicago Poems*. Over the next six years, three more volumes of poetry appeared: *Cornhuskers* (1918), *Smoke and Steel* (1920) and *Slabs of the Sunburnt West* (1922). These collections reflect Sandburg's awareness of America as an increasingly urban nation, and in poems like "Chicago," he celebrates the drive and energy of the working populations of the industrial Midwest.

In 1951, Sandburg won the Pulitzer Prize in poetry for *Complete Poems* (1950). He died July 22, 1967 in Flat Rock, North Carolina.

Contents

HANDFULS

WAR POEMS (1914–1915)

CHICAGO POEMS

Chicago

  Hog Butcher for the World,
  Tool Maker, Stacker of Wheat,
  Player with Railroads and the Nation's Freight Handler;
  Stormy, husky, brawling,
  City of the Big Shoulders:

They tell me you are wicked and I believe them, for I have seen
  your painted women under the gas lamps luring the farm
  boys.
And they tell me you are crooked and I answer: Yes, it is true I have
  seen the gunman kill and go free to kill again.
And they tell me you are brutal and my reply is: On the faces of
  women and children I have seen the marks of wanton hunger.
And having answered so I turn once more to those who sneer at this
  my city, and I give them back the sneer and say to them:
Come and show me another city with lifted head singing so proud
  to be alive and coarse and strong and cunning.
Flinging magnetic curses amid the toil of piling job on job, here is
  a tall bold slugger set vivid against the little soft cities;
Fierce as a dog with tongue lapping for action, cunning as a savage
  pitted against the wilderness,
    Bareheaded,
    Shoveling,
    Wrecking,
    Planning,
    Building, breaking, rebuilding,
Under the smoke, dust all over his mouth, laughing with white
  teeth,
Under the terrible burden of destiny laughing as a young man
  laughs,
Laughing even as an ignorant fighter laughs who has never lost a
  battle,
Bragging and laughing that under his wrist is the pulse, and under
  his ribs the heart of the people,

Laughing!
Laughing the stormy, husky, brawling laughter of Youth, half-
naked, sweating, proud to be Hog Butcher, Tool Maker,
Stacker of Wheat, Player with Railroads and Freight Handler
to the Nation.

Sketch

The shadows of the ships
Rock on the crest
In the low blue lustre
Of the tardy and the soft inrolling tide.

A long brown bar at the dip of the sky
Puts an arm of sand in the span of salt.

The lucid and endless wrinkles
Draw in, lapse and withdraw.
Wavelets crumble and white spent bubbles
Wash on the floor of the beach.

Rocking on the crest
In the low blue lustre
Are the shadows of the ships.

Masses

Among the mountains I wandered and saw blue haze and red crag
and was amazed;
On the beach where the long push under the endless tide maneu-
vers, I stood silent;
Under the stars on the prairie watching the Dipper slant over the
horizon's grass, I was full of thoughts.
Great men, pageants of war and labor, soldiers and workers,
mothers lifting their children — these all I touched, and felt
the solemn thrill of them.
And then one day I got a true look at the Poor, millions of the Poor,
patient and toiling; more patient than crags, tides, and stars;
innumerable, patient as the darkness of night — and all bro-
ken, humble ruins of nations.

Lost

Desolate and lone
All night long on the lake
Where fog trails and mist creeps,
The whistle of a boat
Calls and cries unendingly,
Like some lost child
In tears and trouble
Hunting the harbor's breast
And the harbor's eyes.

The Harbor

Passing through huddled and ugly walls
By doorways where women
Looked from their hunger-deep eyes,
Haunted with shadows of hunger-hands,
Out from the huddled and ugly walls,
I came sudden, at the city's edge,
On a blue burst of lake,
Long lake waves breaking under the sun
On a spray-flung curve of shore;
And a fluttering storm of gulls,
Masses of great gray wings
And flying white bellies
Veering and wheeling free in the open.

They Will Say

Of my city the worst that men will ever say is this:
You took little children away from the sun and the dew,
And the glimmers that played in the grass under the great sky,
And the reckless rain; you put them between walls
To work, broken and smothered, for bread and wages,
To eat dust in their throats and die empty-hearted
For a little handful of pay on a few Saturday nights.

Mill-Doors

You never come back.
I say good-by when I see you going in the doors,
The hopeless open doors that call and wait
And take you then for — how many cents a day?
How many cents for the sleepy eyes and fingers?

I say good-by because I know they tap your wrists,
In the dark, in the silence, day by day,
And all the blood of you drop by drop,
And you are old before you are young.
　　　You never come back.

Halsted Street Car

　　　Come you, cartoonists,
　　　Hang on a strap with me here
　　　At seven o'clock in the morning
　　　On a Halsted street car.

　　　　　Take your pencils
　　　　　And draw these faces.

Try with your pencils for these crooked faces,
That pig-sticker in one corner — his mouth —
That overall factory girl — her loose cheeks.

　　　　　Find for your pencils
　　　　　A way to mark your memory
　　　　　Of tired empty faces.

　　　　　After their night's sleep,
　　　　　In the moist dawn
　　　　　And cool daybreak,
　　　　　　Faces
　　　　　Tired of wishes,
　　　　　Empty of dreams.

Clark Street Bridge

Dust of the feet
And dust of the wheels,
Wagons and people going,
All day feet and wheels.

Now . . .
. . . Only stars and mist
A lonely policeman,
Two cabaret dancers,
Stars and mist again,
No more feet or wheels,
No more dust and wagons.

Voices of dollars
And drops of blood
. . . . .
Voices of broken hearts,
. . . Voices singing, singing,
. . . Silver voices, singing,
Softer than the stars,
Softer than the mist.

Passers-by

Passers-by,
Out of your many faces
Flash memories to me
Now at the day end
Away from the sidewalks
Where your shoe soles traveled
And your voices rose and blent
To form the city's afternoon roar
Hindering an old silence.

Passers-by,
I remember lean ones among you,
Throats in the clutch of a hope,
Lips written over with strivings,
Mouths that kiss only for love,
Records of great wishes slept with,
    Held long
And prayed and toiled for:

    Yes,
Written on
Your mouths
And your throats
I read them
When you passed by.

The Walking Man of Rodin

Legs hold a torso away from the earth.
And a regular high poem of legs is here.
Powers of bone and cord raise a belly and lungs
Out of ooze and over the loam where eyes look and ears hear
And arms have a chance to hammer and shoot and run motors.
        You make us
        Proud of our legs, old man.

And you left off the head here,
The skull found always crumbling neighbor of the ankles.

Subway

Down between the walls of shadow
Where the iron laws insist,
    The hunger voices mock.

The worn wayfaring men
With the hunched and humble shoulders,
    Throw their laughter into toil.

The Shovel Man

    On the street
Slung on his shoulder is a handle half way across,
Tied in a big knot on the scoop of cast iron
Are the overalls faded from sun and rain in the ditches;
Spatter of dry clay sticking yellow on his left sleeve
       And a flimsy shirt open at the throat,
       I know him for a shovel man,
       A dago working for a dollar six bits a day
And a dark-eyed woman in the old country dreams of him for one
    of the world's ready men with a pair of fresh lips and a kiss
    better than all the wild grapes that ever grew in Tuscany.

A Teamster's Farewell

Sobs En Route to a Penitentiary

Good-by now to the streets and the clash of wheels and locking
    hubs,
The sun coming on the brass buckles and harness knobs,
The muscles of the horses sliding under their heavy haunches,
Good-by now to the traffic policeman and his whistle,
The smash of the iron hoof on the stones,
All the crazy wonderful slamming roar of the street —
O God, there's noises I'm going to be hungry for.

Fish Crier

I know a Jew fish crier down on Maxwell Street with a voice like a
    north wind blowing over corn stubble in January.
He dangles herring before prospective customers·evincing a joy
    identical with that of Pavlowa dancing.
His face is that of a man terribly glad to be selling fish, terribly glad
    that God made fish, and customers to whom he may call his
    wares from a pushcart.

Picnic Boat

Sunday night and the park policemen tell each other it is dark as a
    stack of black cats on Lake Michigan.
A big picnic boat comes home to Chicago from the peach farms of
    Saugatuck.
Hundreds of electric bulbs break the night's darkness, a flock of red
    and yellow birds with wings at a standstill.
Running along the deck railings are festoons and leaping in curves
    are loops of light from prow and stern to the tall smokestacks.
Over the hoarse crunch of waves at my pier comes a hoarse answer
    in the rhythmic oompa of the brasses playing a Polish folk-
    song for the home-comers.

Happiness

I asked professors who teach the meaning of life to tell me what is
    happiness.
And I went to famous executives who boss the work of thousands of
    men.
They all shook their heads and gave me a smile as though I was
    trying to fool with them.
And then one Sunday afternoon I wandered out along the Des-
    plaines river
And I saw a crowd of Hungarians under the trees with their women
    and children and a keg of beer and an accordion.

Muckers

Twenty men stand watching the muckers.
        Stabbing the sides of the ditch
        Where clay gleams yellow,
        Driving the blades of their shovels
        Deeper and deeper for the new gas mains,
        Wiping sweat off their faces

With red bandanas.
The muckers work on . . . pausing . . . to pull
Their boots out of suckholes where they slosh.

    Of the twenty looking on
Ten murmur, "O, it's a hell of a job,"
Ten others, "Jesus, I wish I had the job."

Blacklisted

Why shall I keep the old name?
What is a name anywhere anyway?
A name is a cheap thing all fathers and mothers leave each child:
A job is a job and I want to live, so
Why does God Almighty or anybody else care whether I take a new
    name to go by?

Graceland

    Tomb of a millionaire,
    A multi-millionaire, ladies and gentlemen,
    Place of the dead where they spend every year
    The usury of twenty-five thousand dollars
        For upkeep and flowers
    To keep fresh the memory of the dead.
    The merchant prince gone to dust
    Commanded in his written will
    Over the signed name of his last testament
    Twenty-five thousand dollars be set aside
    For roses, lilacs, hydrangeas, tulips,
    For perfume and color, sweetness of remembrance
    Around his last long home.

(A hundred cash girls want nickels to go to the movies to-night.
In the back stalls of a hundred saloons, women are at tables
Drinking with men or waiting for men jingling loose silver dollars
    in their pockets.

In a hundred furnished rooms is a girl who sells silk or dress goods
>   or leather stuff for six dollars a week wages
And when she pulls on her stockings in the morning she is reckless
>   about God and the newspapers and the police, the talk of her
>   home town or the name people call her.)

Child of the Romans

The dago shovelman sits by the railroad track
Eating a noon meal of bread and bologna.
>   A train whirls by, and men and women at tables
>   Alive with red roses and yellow jonquils,
>   Eat steaks running with brown gravy,
>   Strawberries and cream, eclaires and coffee.
The dago shovelman finishes the dry bread and bologna,
Washes it down with a dipper from the water-boy,
And goes back to the second half of a ten-hour day's work
Keeping the road-bed so the roses and jonquils
Shake hardly at all in the cut glass vases
Standing slender on the tables in the dining cars.

The Right to Grief

To Certain Poets About to Die

Take your fill of intimate remorse, perfumed sorrow,
Over the dead child of a millionaire,
And the pity of Death refusing any check on the bank
Which the millionaire might order his secretary to scratch off
And get cashed.

>   Very well,
You for your grief and I for mine.
Let me have a sorrow my own if I want to.

I shall cry over the dead child of a stockyards hunky.
His job is sweeping blood off the floor.
He gets a dollar seventy cents a day when he works
And it's many tubs of blood he shoves out with a broom day by day.

Now his three year old daughter
Is in a white coffin that cost him a week's wages.
Every Saturday night he will pay the undertaker fifty cents till the
    debt is wiped out.

The hunky and his wife and the kids
Cry over the pinched face almost at peace in the white box.
They remember it was scrawny and ran up high doctor bills.
They are glad it is gone for the rest of the family now will have more
    to eat and wear.

Yet before the majesty of Death they cry around the coffin
And wipe their eyes with red bandanas and sob when the priest
    says, "God have mercy on us all."

I have a right to feel my throat choke about this.
You take your grief and I mine — see?
To-morrow there is no funeral and the hunky goes back to his job
    sweeping blood off the floor at a dollar seventy cents a day.
All he does all day long is keep on shoving hog blood ahead of him
    with a broom.

Mag

I wish to God I never saw you, Mag.
I wish you never quit your job and came along with me.
I wish we never bought a license and a white dress
For you to get married in the day we ran off to a minister
And told him we would love each other and take care of each other
Always and always long as the sun and the rain lasts anywhere.
Yes, I'm wishing now you lived somewhere away from here
And I was a bum on the bumpers a thousand miles away dead
    broke.
        I wish the kids had never come
        And rent and coal and clothes to pay for
        And a grocery man calling for cash,
        Every day cash for beans and prunes.
        I wish to God I never saw you, Mag.
        I wish to God the kids had never come.

Onion Days

Mrs. Gabrielle Giovannitti comes along Peoria Street every morn-
 ing at nine o'clock
With kindling wood piled on top of her head, her eyes looking
 straight ahead to find the way for her old feet.
Her daughter-in-law, Mrs. Pietro Giovannitti, whose husband was
 killed in a tunnel explosion through the negligence of a
 fellow-servant,
Works ten hours a day, sometimes twelve, picking onions for Jasper
 on the Bowmanville road.
She takes a street car at half-past five in the morning, Mrs. Pietro
 Giovannitti does,
And gets back from Jasper's with cash for her day's work, between
 nine and ten o'clock at night.
Last week she got eight cents a box, Mrs. Pietro Giovannitti,
 picking onions for Jasper,
But this week Jasper dropped the pay to six cents a box because so
 many women and girls were answering the ads in the *Daily
 News*.
Jasper belongs to an Episcopal church in Ravenswood and on
 certain Sundays
He enjoys chanting the Nicene creed with his daughters on each
 side of him joining their voices with his.
If the preacher repeats old sermons of a Sunday, Jasper's mind
 wanders to his 700-acre farm and how he can make it produce
 more efficiently
And sometimes he speculates on whether he could word an ad in
 the *Daily News* so it would bring more women and girls out to
 his farm and reduce operating costs.
Mrs. Pietro Giovannitti is far from desperate about life; her joy is in
 a child she knows will arrive to her in three months.
And now while these are the pictures for today there are other
 pictures of the Giovannitti people I could give you for to-
 morrow,
And how some of them go to the county agent on winter mornings
 with their baskets for beans and cornmeal and molasses.
I listen to fellows saying here's good stuff for a novel or it might be
 worked up into a good play.

I say there's no dramatist living can put old Mrs. Gabrielle Giovan-
nitti into a play with that kindling wood piled on top of her
head coming along Peoria Street nine o'clock in the morning.

Population Drifts

New-mown hay smell and wind of the plain made her a woman
whose ribs had the power of the hills in them and her hands
were tough for work and there was passion for life in her
womb.

She and her man crossed the ocean and the years that marked their
faces saw them haggling with landlords and grocers while six
children played on the stones and prowled in the garbage
cans.

One child coughed its lungs away, two more have adenoids and
can neither talk nor run like their mother, one is in jail, two
have jobs in a box factory

And as they fold the pasteboard, they wonder what the wishing is
and the wistful glory in them that flutters faintly when the
glimmer of spring comes on the air or the green of summer
turns brown:

They do not know it is the new-mown hay smell calling and the
wind of the plain praying for them to come back and take hold
of life again with tough hands and with passion.

Cripple

Once when I saw a cripple
Gasping slowly his last days with the white plague,
Looking from hollow eyes, calling for air,
Desperately gesturing with wasted hands
In the dark and dust of a house down in a slum,
I said to myself
I would rather have been a tall sunflower
Living in a country garden
Lifting a golden-brown face to the summer,
Rain-washed and dew-misted,

Mixed with the poppies and ranking hollyhocks,
And wonderingly watching night after night
The clear silent processionals of stars.

A Fence

Now the stone house on the lake front is finished and the workmen
     are beginning the fence.
The palings are made of iron bars with steel points that can stab the
     life out of any man who falls on them.
As a fence, it is a masterpiece, and will shut off the rabble and all
     vagabonds and hungry men and all wandering children look-
     ing for a place to play.
Passing through the bars and over the steel points will go nothing
     except Death and the Rain and To-morrow.

Anna Imroth

Cross the hands over the breast here — so.
Straighten the legs a little more — so.
And call for the wagon to come and take her home.
Her mother will cry some and so will her sisters and brothers.
But all of the others got down and they are safe and this is the only
     one of the factory girls who wasn't lucky in making the jump
     when the fire broke.
It is the hand of God and the lack of fire escapes.

Working Girls

The working girls in the morning are going to work — long lines of
     them afoot amid the downtown stores and factories, thousands
     with little brick-shaped lunches wrapped in newspapers under
     their arms.
Each morning as I move through this river of young-woman life I
     feel a wonder about where it is all going, so many with a peach
     bloom of young years on them and laughter of red lips and

memories in their eyes of dances the night before and plays and walks.

Green and gray streams run side by side in a river and so here are always the others, those who have been over the way, the women who know each one the end of life's gamble for her, the meaning and the clew, the how and the why of the dances and the arms that passed around their waists and the fingers that played in their hair.

Faces go by written over: "I know it all, I know where the bloom and the laughter go and I have memories," and the feet of these move slower and they have wisdom where the others have beauty.

So the green and the gray move in the early morning on the downtown streets.

Mamie

Mamie beat her head against the bars of a little Indiana town and dreamed of romance and big things off somewhere the way the railroad trains all ran.

She could see the smoke of the engines get lost down where the streaks of steel flashed in the sun and when the newspapers came in on the morning mail she knew there was a big Chicago far off, where all the trains ran.

She got tired of the barber shop boys and the post office chatter and the church gossip and the old pieces the band played on the Fourth of July and Decoration Day

And sobbed at her fate and beat her head against the bars and was going to kill herself

When the thought came to her that if she was going to die she might as well die struggling for a clutch of romance among the streets of Chicago.

She has a job now at six dollars a week in the basement of the Boston Store

And even now she beats her head against the bars in the same old way and wonders if there is a bigger place the railroads run to from Chicago where maybe there is

               romance
               and big things
               and real dreams
               that never go smash.

Personality

Musings of a Police Reporter in the Identification Bureau

You have loved forty women, but you have only one thumb.
You have led a hundred secret lives, but you mark only one thumb.
You go round the world and fight in a thousand wars and win all the
    world's honors, but when you come back home the print of
    the one thumb your mother gave you is the same print of
    thumb you had in the old home when your mother kissed you
    and said good-by.
Out of the whirling womb of time come millions of men and their
    feet crowd the earth and they cut one anothers' throats for
    room to stand and among them all are not two thumbs alike.
Somewhere is a Great God of Thumbs who can tell the inside story
    of this.

Cumulatives

Storms have beaten on this point of land
And ships gone to wreck here
            and the passers-by remember it
            with talk on the deck at night
            as they near it.

Fists have beaten on the face of this old prize-fighter
And his battles have held the sporting pages
            and on the street they indicate him with their
            right fore-finger as one who once wore
            a championship belt.

A hundred stories have been published and a thousand rumored
About why this tall dark man has divorced two beautiful young
        women
And married a third who resembles the first two
            and they shake their heads and say, "There he goes,"
            when he passes by in sunny weather or in rain
            along the city streets.

To Certain Journeymen

Undertakers, hearse drivers, grave diggers,
I speak to you as one not afraid of your business.

You handle dust going to a long country,
You know the secret behind your job is the same whether you lower
the coffin with modern, automatic machinery, well-oiled and
noiseless, or whether the body is laid in by naked hands and
then covered by the shovels.

Your day's work is done with laughter many days of the year,
And you earn a living by those who say good-by today in thin
whispers.

Chamfort

There's Chamfort. He's a sample.
Locked himself in his library with a gun,
Shot off his nose and shot out his right eye.
And this Chamfort knew how to write
And thousands read his books on how to live,
But he himself didn't know
How to die by force of his own hand — see?
They found him a red pool on the carpet
Cool as an April forenoon,
Talking and talking gay maxims and grim epigrams.
Well, he wore bandages over his nose and right eye,
Drank coffee and chatted many years
With men and women who loved him
Because he laughed and daily dared Death:
"Come and take me."

Limited

I am riding on a limited express, one of the crack trains of the
    nation.
Hurtling across the prairie into blue haze and dark air go fifteen all-
    steel coaches holding a thousand people.
(All the coaches shall be scrap and rust and all the men and women
    laughing in the diners and sleepers shall pass to ashes.)
I ask a man in the smoker where he is going and he answers:
    "Omaha."

The Has-Been

A stone face higher than six horses stood five thousand years gazing
    at the world seeming to clutch a secret.
A boy passes and throws a niggerhead that chips off the end of the
    nose from the stone face; he lets fly a mud ball that spatters the
    right eye and cheek of the old looker-on.
The boy laughs and goes whistling "ee-ee-ee ee-ee-ee." The stone
    face stands silent, seeming to clutch a secret.

In a Back Alley

Remembrance for a great man is this.
The newsies are pitching pennies.
And on the copper disk is the man's face.
Dead lover of boys, what do you ask for now?

A Coin

Your western heads here cast on money,
You are the two that fade away together,
        Partners in the mist.

Lunging buffalo shoulder,
Lean Indian face,
We who come after where you are gone
Salute your forms on the new nickel.

You are
To us:
The past.

Runners
On the prairie:
Good-by.

Dynamiter

I sat with a dynamiter at supper in a German saloon eating steak
and onions.
And he laughed and told stories of his wife and children and the
cause of labor and the working class.
It was laughter of an unshakable man knowing life to be a rich and
red-blooded thing.
Yes, his laugh rang like the call of gray birds filled with a glory of joy
ramming their winged flight through a rain storm.
His name was in many newspapers as an enemy of the nation and
few keepers of churches or schools would open their doors to
him.
Over the steak and onions not a word was said of his deep days and
nights as a dynamiter.
Only I always remember him as a lover of life, a lover of children, a
lover of all free, reckless laughter everywhere — lover of red
hearts and red blood the world over.

Ice Handler

I know an ice handler who wears a flannel shirt with pearl buttons
the size of a dollar,
And he lugs a hundred-pound hunk into a saloon icebox, helps
himself to cold ham and rye bread,

Tells the bartender it's hotter than yesterday and will be hotter yet
    to-morrow, by Jesus,
And is on his way with his head in the air and a hard pair of fists.
He spends a dollar or so every Saturday night on a two hundred
    pound woman who washes dishes in the Hotel Morrison.
He remembers when the union was organized he broke the noses
    of two scabs and loosened the nuts so the wheels came off six
    different wagons one morning, and he came around and
    watched the ice melt in the street.
All he was sorry for was one of the scabs bit him on the knuckles of
    the right hand so they bled when he came around to the
    saloon to tell the boys about it.

Jack

Jack was a swarthy, swaggering son-of-a-gun.
He worked thirty years on the railroad, ten hours a day, and his
    hands were tougher than sole leather.
He married a tough woman and they had eight children and the
    woman died and the children grew up and went away and
    wrote the old man every two years.
He died in the poorhouse sitting on a bench in the sun telling
    reminiscences to other old men whose women were dead and
    children scattered.
There was joy on his face when he died as there was joy on his face
    when he lived — he was a swarthy, swaggering son-of-a-gun.

Fellow Citizens

I drank musty ale at the Illinois Athletic Club with the millionaire
    manufacturer of Green River butter one night
And his face had the shining light of an old-time Quaker, he spoke
    of a beautiful daughter, and I knew he had a peace and a
    happiness up his sleeve somewhere.
Then I heard Jim Kirch make a speech to the Advertising Associa-
    tion on the trade resources of South America.

And the way he lighted a three-for-a-nickel stogie and cocked it at
an angle regardless of the manners of our best people,
I knew he had a clutch on a real happiness even though some of
the reporters on his newspaper say he is the living double of
Jack London's Sea Wolf.
In the mayor's office the mayor himself told me he was happy
though it is a hard job to satisfy all the office-seekers and eat all
the dinners he is asked to eat.
Down in Gilpin Place, near Hull House, was a man with his jaw
wrapped for a bad toothache,
And he had it all over the butter millionaire, Jim Kirch and the
mayor when it came to happiness.
He is a maker of accordions and guitars and not only makes them
from start to finish, but plays them after he makes them.
And he had a guitar of mahogany with a walnut bottom he offered
for seven dollars and a half if I wanted it,
And another just like it, only smaller, for six dollars, though he
never mentioned the price till I asked him,
And he stated the price in a sorry way, as though the music and the
make of an instrument count for a million times more than
the price in money.
I thought he had a real soul and knew a lot about God.
There was light in his eyes of one who has conquered sorrow in so
far as sorrow is conquerable or worth conquering.
Anyway he is the only Chicago citizen I was jealous of that day.
He played a dance they play in some parts of Italy when the harvest
of grapes is over and the wine presses are ready for work.

Nigger

I am the nigger.
Singer of songs,
Dancer . . .
Softer than fluff of cotton . . .
Harder than dark earth
Roads beaten in the sun
By the bare feet of slaves . . .
Foam of teeth . . . breaking crash of laughter . . .
Red love of the blood of woman,

White love of the tumbling pickaninnies. . .
Lazy love of the banjo thrum. . .
Sweated and driven for the harvest-wage,
Loud laugher with hands like hams,
Fists toughened on the handles,
Smiling the slumber dreams of old jungles,
Crazy as the sun and dew and dripping, heaving life of the jungle,
Brooding and muttering with memories of shackles:
> I am the nigger.
> Look at me.
> I am the nigger.

Two Neighbors

Faces of two eternities keep looking at me.
One is Omar Khayam and the red stuff
> wherein men forget yesterday and to-morrow
> and remember only the voices and songs,
> the stories, newspapers and fights of today.
One is Louis Cornaro and a slim trick
> of slow, short meals across slow, short years,
> letting Death open the door only in slow, short inches.
I have a neighbor who swears by Omar.
I have a neighbor who swears by Cornaro.
> > Both are happy.
Faces of two eternities keep looking at me.
> > Let them look.

Style

Style — go ahead talking about style.
You can tell where a man gets his style just
> as you can tell where Pavlowa got her legs
> or Ty Cobb his batting eye.

> Go on talking.
Only don't take my style away.
> It's my face.

Maybe no good
        but anyway, my face.
I talk with it, I sing with it, I see, taste and feel with it,
    I know why I want to keep it.

Kill my style
            and you break Pavlowa's legs,
            and you blind Ty Cobb's batting eye.

To Beachey, 1912

Riding against the east,
A veering, steady shadow
Purrs the motor-call
Of the man-bird
Ready with the death-laughter
In his throat
And in his heart always
The love of the big blue beyond.

Only a man,
A far fleck of shadow on the east
Sitting at ease
With his hands on a wheel
And around him the large gray wings.
Hold him, great soft wings,
Keep and deal kindly, O wings,
With the cool, calm shadow at the wheel.

Under a Hat Rim

While the hum and the hurry
Of passing footfalls
Beat in my ear like the restless surf
Of a wind-blown sea,
A soul came to me
Out of the look on a face.

Eyes like a lake
Where a storm-wind roams
Caught me from under
The rim of a hat.
     I thought of a midsea wreck
     and bruised fingers clinging
     to a broken state-room door.

In a Breath

To the Williamson Brothers

High noon. White sun flashes on the Michigan Avenue asphalt.
    Drum of hoofs and whirr of motors. Women trapsing along in
    flimsy clothes catching play of sun-fire to their skin and eyes.

Inside the playhouse are movies from under the sea. From the heat
    of pavements and the dust of sidewalks, passers-by go in a
    breath to be witnesses of large cool sponges, large cool fishes,
    large cool valleys and ridges of coral spread silent in the soak
    of the ocean floor thousands of years.

A naked swimmer dives. A knife in his right hand shoots a streak at
    the throat of a shark. The tail of the shark lashes. One swing
    would kill the swimmer . . . Soon the knife goes into the soft
    underneck of the veering fish . . . Its mouthful of teeth, each
    tooth a dagger itself, set row on row, glistens when the shud-
    dering, yawning cadaver is hauled up by the brothers of the
    swimmer.

Outside in the street is the murmur and singing of life in the sun —
    horses, motors, women trapsing along in flimsy clothes, play
    of sun-fire in their blood.

Bath

A man saw the whole world as a grinning skull and cross-bones.
The rose flesh of life shriveled from all faces. Nothing counts.
Everything is a fake. Dust to dust and ashes to ashes and then an old

darkness and a useless silence. So he saw it all. Then he went to a Mischa Elman concert. Two hours waves of sound beat on his eardrums. Music washed something or other inside him. Music broke down and rebuilt something or other in his head and heart. He joined in five encores for the young Russian Jew with the fiddle. When he got outside his heels hit the sidewalk a new way. He was the same man in the same world as before. Only there was a singing fire and a climb of roses everlastingly over the world he looked on.

Bronzes

I

The bronze General Grant riding a bronze horse in Lincoln Park
Shrivels in the sun by day when the motor cars whirr by in long
    processions going somewhere to keep appointment for dinner
    and matineés and buying and selling
Though in the dusk and nightfall when high waves are piling
On the slabs of the promenade along the lake shore near by
I have seen the general dare the combers come closer
And make to ride his bronze horse out into the hoofs and guns of
    the storm.

II

I cross Lincoln Park on a winter night when the snow is falling.
Lincoln in bronze stands among the white lines of snow, his bronze
    forehead meeting soft echoes of the newsies crying forty thou-
    sand men are dead along the Yser, his bronze ears listening to
    the mumbled roar of the city at his bronze feet.
A lithe Indian on a bronze pony, Shakespeare seated with long legs
    in bronze, Garibaldi in a bronze cape, they hold places in the
    cold, lonely snow to-night on their pedestals and so they will
    hold them past midnight and into the dawn.

Dunes

What do we see here in the sand dunes of the white moon alone
    with our thoughts, Bill,
Alone with our dreams, Bill, soft as the women tying scarves around
    their heads dancing,
Alone with a picture and a picture coming one after the other of all
    the dead,
The dead more than all these grains of sand one by one piled here
    in the moon,
Piled against the sky-line taking shapes like the hand of the wind
    wanted,
What do we see here, Bill, outside of what the wise men beat their
    heads on,
Outside of what the poets cry for and the soldiers drive on headlong
    and leave their skulls in the sun for — what, Bill?

On the Way

Little one, you have been buzzing in the books,
Flittering in the newspapers and drinking beer with lawyers
And amid the educated men of the clubs you have been getting an
    earful of speech from trained tongues.
Take an earful from me once, go with me on a hike
Along sand stretches on the great inland sea here
And while the eastern breeze blows on us and the restless surge
Of the lake waves on the breakwater breaks with an ever fresh
    monotone,
Let us ask ourselves: What is truth? what do you or I know?
How much do the wisest of the world's men know about where the
    massed human procession is going?

You have heard the mob laughed at?
I ask you: Is not the mob rough as the mountains are rough?
And all things human rise from the mob and relapse and rise again
    as rain to the sea?

Ready to Kill

Ten minutes now I have been looking at this.
I have gone by here before and wondered about it.
This is a bronze memorial of a famous general
Riding horseback with a flag and a sword and a revolver on him.
I want to smash the whole thing into a pile of junk to be hauled
     away to the scrap yard.
I put it straight to you,
After the farmer, the miner, the shop man, the factory hand, the
     fireman and the teamster,
Have all been remembered with bronze memorials,
Shaping them on the job of getting all of us
Something to eat and something to wear,
When they stack a few silhouettes
          Against the sky
          Here in the park,
And show the real huskies that are doing the work of the world, and
     feeding people instead of butchering them,
Then maybe I will stand here
And look easy at this general of the army holding a flag in the air,
And riding like hell on horseback
Ready to kill anybody that gets in his way,
Ready to run the red blood and slush the bowels of men all over the
     sweet new grass of the prairie.

To a Contemporary Bunkshooter

You come along . . . tearing your shirt . . . yelling about Jesus.
          Where do you get that stuff?
          What do you know about Jesus?
Jesus had a way of talking soft and outside of a few bankers and
     higher-ups among the con men of Jerusalem everybody liked
     to have this Jesus around because he never made any fake
     passes and everything he said went and he helped the sick and
     gave the people hope.

You come along squirting words at us, shaking your fist and calling
  us all dam fools so fierce the froth slobbers over your lips . . .
  always blabbing we're all going to hell straight off and you
  know all about it.

I've read Jesus' words. I know what he said. You don't throw any
  scare into me. I've got your number. I know how much you
  know about Jesus.

He never came near clean people or dirty people but they felt
  cleaner because he came along. It was your crowd of bankers
  and business men and lawyers hired the sluggers and mur-
  derers who put Jesus out of the running.

I say the same bunch backing you nailed the nails into the hands of
  this Jesus of Nazareth. He had lined up against him the same
  crooks and strong-arm men now lined up with you paying
  your way.

This Jesus was good to look at, smelled good, listened good. He
  threw out something fresh and beautiful from the skin of his
  body and the touch of his hands wherever he passed along.

You slimy bunkshooter, you put a smut on every human blossom in
  reach of your rotten breath belching about hell-fire and hic-
  cupping about this Man who lived a clean life in Galilee.

When are you going to quit making the carpenters build emer-
  gency hospitals for women and girls driven crazy with
  wrecked nerves from your gibberish about Jesus — I put it to
  you again: Where do you get that stuff; what do you know
  about Jesus?

Go ahead and bust all the chairs you want to. Smash a whole
  wagon load of furniture at every performance. Turn sixty
  somersaults and stand on your nutty head. If it wasn't for the
  way you scare the women and kids I'd feel sorry for you and
  pass the hat.

I like to watch a good four-flusher work, but not when he starts
  people puking and calling for the doctors.

I like a man that's got nerve and can pull off a great original
  performance, but you — you're only a bug-house peddler of
  second-hand gospel — you're only shoving out a phoney imita-
  tion of the goods this Jesus wanted free as air and sunlight.

You tell people living in shanties Jesus is going to fix it up all right

with them by giving them mansions in the skies after they're
dead and the worms have eaten 'em.

You tell $6 a week department store girls all they need is Jesus; you
take a steel trust wop, dead without having lived, gray and
shrunken at forty years of age, and you tell him to look at Jesus
on the cross and he'll be all right.

You tell poor people they don't need any more money on pay day
and even if it's fierce to be out of a job, Jesus'll fix that up all
right, all right—all they gotta do is take Jesus the way you say.

I'm telling you Jesus wouldn't stand for the stuff you're handing
out. Jesus played it different. The bankers and lawyers of
Jerusalem got their sluggers and murderers to go after Jesus
just because Jesus wouldn't play their game. He didn't sit in
with the big thieves.

I don't want a lot of gab from a bunkshooter in my religion.

I won't take my religion from any man who never works except
with his mouth and never cherishes any memory except the
face of the woman on the American silver dollar.

I ask you to come through and show me where you're pouring out
the blood of your life.

I've been to this suburb of Jerusalem they call Golgotha, where
they nailed Him, and I know if the story is straight it was real
blood ran from His hands and the nail-holes, and it was real
blood spurted in red drops where the spear of the Roman
soldier rammed in between the ribs of this Jesus of Nazareth.

Skyscraper

By day the skyscraper looms in the smoke and sun and has a soul.

Prairie and valley, streets of the city, pour people into it and they
mingle among its twenty floors and are poured out again back
to the streets, prairies and valleys.

It is the men and women, boys and girls so poured in and out all
day that give the building a soul of dreams and thoughts and
memories.

(Dumped in the sea or fixed in a desert, who would care for the
building or speak its name or ask a policeman the way to it?)

Elevators slide on their cables and tubes catch letters and parcels
and iron pipes carry gas and water in and sewage out.
Wires climb with secrets, carry light and carry words, and tell
terrors and profits and loves — curses of men grappling plans
of business and questions of women in plots of love.

Hour by hour the caissons reach down to the rock of the earth and
hold the building to a turning planet.
Hour by hour the girders play as ribs and reach out and hold
together the stone walls and floors.
Hour by hour the hand of the mason and the stuff of the mortar
clinch the pieces and parts to the shape an architect voted.
Hour by hour the sun and the rain, the air and the rust, and the
press of time running into centuries, play on the building
inside and out and use it.

Men who sunk the pilings and mixed the mortar are laid in graves
where the wind whistles a wild song without words
And so are men who strung the wires and fixed the pipes and tubes
and those who saw it rise floor by floor.
Souls of them all are here, even the hod carrier begging at back
doors hundreds of miles away and the bricklayer who went to
state's prison for shooting another man while drunk.
(One man fell from a girder and broke his neck at the end of a
straight plunge — he is here — his soul has gone into the stones
of the building.)

On the office doors from tier to tier — hundreds of names and each
name standing for a face written across with a dead child, a
passionate lover, a driving ambition for a million dollar busi-
ness or a lobster's ease of life.

Behind the signs on the doors they work and the walls tell nothing
from room to room.
Ten-dollar-a-week stenographers take letters from corporation offi-
cers, lawyers, efficiency engineers, and tons of letters go bun-
dled from the building to all ends of the earth.
Smiles and tears of each office girl go into the soul of the building
just the same as the master-men who rule the building.

Hands of clocks turn to noon hours and each floor empties its men
and women who go away and eat and come back to work.

Toward the end of the afternoon all work slackens and all jobs go
    slower as the people feel day closing on them.
One by one the floors are emptied . . . The uniformed elevator
    men are gone. Pails clang . . . Scrubbers work, talking in
    foreign tongues. Broom and water and mop clean from the
    floors human dust and spit, and machine grime of the day.
Spelled in electric fire on the roof are words telling miles of houses
    and people where to buy a thing for money. The sign speaks
    till midnight.

Darkness on the hallways. Voices echo. Silence holds . . . Watch-
    men walk slow from floor to floor and try the doors. Revolvers
    bulge from their hip pockets . . . Steel safes stand in corners.
    Money is stacked in them.
A young watchman leans at a window and sees the lights of barges
    butting their way across a harbor, nets of red and white lan-
    terns in a railroad yard, and a span of glooms splashed with
    lines of white and blurs of crosses and clusters over the sleep-
    ing city.
By night the skyscraper looms in the smoke and the stars and has a
    soul.

HANDFULS

Fog

The fog comes
on little cat feet.

It sits looking
over harbor and city
on silent haunches
and then moves on.

Pool

Out of the fire
Came a man sunken
To less than cinders,
A tea-cup of ashes or so.
And I,
The gold in the house,
Writhed into a stiff pool.

Jan Kubelik

Your bow swept over a string, and a long low note quivered to the
    air.
(A mother of Bohemia sobs over a new child perfect learning to
    suck milk.)

Your bow ran fast over all the high strings fluttering and wild.
(All the girls in Bohemia are laughing on a Sunday afternoon in the
    hills with their lovers.)

Choose

The single clenched fist lifted and ready,
Or the open asking hand held out and waiting.
                    Choose:
For we meet by one or the other.

Crimson

Crimson is the slow smolder of the cigar end I hold,
Gray is the ash that stiffens and covers all silent the fire.
(A great man I know is dead and while he lies in his coffin a gone
    flame I sit here in cumbering shadows and smoke and watch
    my thoughts come and go.)

Whitelight

Your whitelight flashes the frost to-night
Moon of the purple and silent west.
Remember me one of your lovers of dreams.

Flux

Sand of the sea runs red
Where the sunset reaches and quivers.
Sand of the sea runs yellow
Where the moon slants and wavers.

Kin

Brother, I am fire
Surging under the ocean floor.
I shall never meet you, brother—

Not for years, anyhow;
Maybe thousands of years, brother.
Then I will warm you,
Hold you close, wrap you in circles,
Use you and change you —
Maybe thousands of years, brother.

White Shoulders

Your white shoulders
    I remember
And your shrug of laughter.

    Low laughter
    Shaken slow
From your white shoulders.

Losses

I have love
And a child,
A banjo
And shadows.
(Losses of God,
All will go
And one day
We will hold
Only the shadows.)

Troths

Yellow dust on a bumble
    bee's wing,
Gray lights in a woman's
    asking eyes,

Red ruins in the changing
    sunset embers:
I take you and pile high
    the memories.
Death will break her claws
    on some I keep.

WAR POEMS
(1914–1915)

Killers

I am singing to you
Soft as a man with a dead child speaks;
Hard as a man in handcuffs,
Held where he cannot move:

   Under the sun
Are sixteen million men,
Chosen for shining teeth,
Sharp eyes, hard legs,
And a running of young warm blood in their wrists.

   And a red juice runs on the green grass;
And a red juice soaks the dark soil.
And the sixteen million are killing . . . and killing and killing.

   I never forget them day or night:
They beat on my head for memory of them;
They pound on my heart and I cry back to them,
To their homes and women, dreams and games.

   I wake in the night and smell the trenches,
And hear the low stir of sleepers in lines—
Sixteen million sleepers and pickets in the dark:
Some of them long sleepers for always,
Some of them tumbling to sleep to-morrow for always,
Fixed in the drag of the world's heartbreak,
Eating and drinking, toiling . . . on a long job of killing.
   Sixteen million men.

Among the Red Guns

After waking at dawn one morning when the wind sang low
among dry leaves in an elm

Among the red guns,
In the hearts of soldiers
Running free blood
In the long, long campaign:
    Dreams go on.

Among the leather saddles,
In the heads of soldiers
Heavy in the wracks and kills
Of all straight fighting:
    Dreams go on.

Among the hot muzzles,
In the hands of soldiers
Brought from flesh-folds of women —
Soft amid the blood and crying —
In all your hearts and heads
Among the guns and saddles and muzzles:

    Dreams,
Dreams go on,
Out of the dead on their backs,
Broken and no use any more:
Dreams of the way and the end go on.

Iron

Guns,
Long, steel guns,
Pointed from the war ships
In the name of the war god.
Straight, shining, polished guns,
Clambered over with jackies in white blouses,
Glory of tan faces, tousled hair, white teeth,

Laughing lithe jackies in white blouses,
Sitting on the guns singing war songs, war chanties.

Shovels,
Broad, iron shovels,
Scooping out oblong vaults,
Loosening turf and leveling sod.

    I ask you
    To witness —
    The shovel is brother to the gun.

Murmurings in a Field Hospital

*[They picked him up in the grass where he had lain two days in
    the rain with a piece of shrapnel in his lungs.]*

Come to me only with playthings now . . .
A picture of a singing woman with blue eyes
Standing at a fence of hollyhocks, poppies and sunflowers . . .
Or an old man I remember sitting with children telling stories
Of days that never happened anywhere in the world . . .

No more iron cold and real to handle,
Shaped for a drive straight ahead.
Bring me only beautiful useless things.
Only old home things touched at sunset in the quiet . . .
And at the window one day in summer
Yellow of the new crock of butter
Stood against the red of new climbing roses . . .
And the world was all playthings.

Statistics

Napoleon shifted,
Restless in the old sarcophagus
And murmured to a watchguard:
"Who goes there?"

"Twenty-one million men,
Soldiers, armies, guns,
Twenty-one million
Afoot, horseback,
In the air,
Under the sea."
And Napoleon turned to his sleep:
"It is not my world answering;
It is some dreamer who knows not
The world I marched in
From Calais to Moscow."
And he slept on
In the old sarcophagus
While the aëroplanes
Droned their motors
Between Napoleon's mausoleum
And the cool night stars.

Fight

Red drips from my chin where I have been eating.
Not all the blood, nowhere near all, is wiped off my mouth.

Clots of red mess my hair
And the tiger, the buffalo, know how.

I was a killer.
        Yes, I am a killer.

I come from killing.
        I go to more.
I drive red joy ahead of me from killing.
Red gluts and red hungers run in the smears and juices of my
        inside bones:
The child cries for a suck mother and I cry for war.

Buttons

I have been watching the war map slammed up for advertising in
    front of the newspaper office.
Buttons — red and yellow buttons — blue and black buttons — are
    shoved back and forth across the map.

A laughing young man, sunny with freckles,
Climbs a ladder, yells a joke to somebody in the crowd,
And then fixes a yellow button one inch west
And follows the yellow button with a black button one inch west.

(Ten thousand men and boys twist on their bodies in a red soak
    along a river edge,
Gasping of wounds, calling for water, some rattling death in their
    throats.)
Who would guess what it cost to move two buttons one inch on the
    war map here in front of the newspaper office where the
    freckle-faced young man is laughing to us?

And They Obey

Smash down the cities.
Knock the walls to pieces.
Break the factories and cathedrals, warehouses and homes
Into loose piles of stone and lumber and black burnt wood:
    You are the soldiers and we command you.

Build up the cities.
Set up the walls again.
Put together once more the factories and cathedrals, warehouses
    and homes
Into buildings for life and labor:
    You are workmen and citizens all: We command you.

Jaws

Seven nations stood with their hands on the jaws of death.
It was the first week in August, Nineteen Hundred Fourteen.
I was listening, you were listening, the whole world was listening,
And all of us heard a Voice murmuring:
  "I am the way and the light,
  He that believeth on me
  Shall not perish
  But shall have everlasting life."
Seven nations listening heard the Voice and answered:
  "O Hell!"
The jaws of death began clicking and they go on clicking:
  "O Hell!"

Salvage

Guns on the battle lines have pounded now a year between
  Brussels and Paris.
And, William Morris, when I read your old chapter on the great
  arches and naves and little whimsical corners of the Churches
  of Northern France — Brr-rr!
I'm glad you're a dead man, William Morris, I'm glad you're down
  in the damp and mouldy, only a memory instead of a living
  man — I'm glad you're gone.
You never lied to us, William Morris, you loved the shape of those
  stones piled and carved for you to dream over and wonder
  because workmen got joy of life into them,
Workmen in aprons singing while they hammered, and praying,
  and putting their songs and prayers into the walls and roofs,
  the bastions and cornerstones and gargoyles — all their chil-
  dren and kisses of women and wheat and roses growing.
I say, William Morris, I'm glad you're gone, I'm glad you're a dead
  man.
Guns on the battle lines have pounded a year now between
  Brussels and Paris.

Wars

In the old wars drum of hoofs and the beat of shod feet.
In the new wars hum of motors and the tread of rubber tires.
In the wars to come silent wheels and whirr of rods not yet dreamed
out in the heads of men.

In the old wars clutches of short swords and jabs into faces with
spears.
In the new wars long range guns and smashed walls, guns running
a spit of metal and men falling in tens and twenties.
In the wars to come new silent deaths, new silent hurlers not yet
dreamed out in the heads of men.

In the old wars kings quarreling and thousands of men following.
In the new wars kings quarreling and millions of men following.
In the wars to come kings kicked under the dust and millions of
men following great causes not yet dreamed out in the heads
of men.

THE ROAD AND THE END

The Road and the End

I shall foot it
Down the roadway in the dusk,
Where shapes of hunger wander
And the fugitives of pain go by.
I shall foot it
In the silence of the morning,
See the night slur into dawn,
Hear the slow great winds arise
Where tall trees flank the way
And shoulder toward the sky.

The broken boulders by the road
Shall not commemorate my ruin.
Regret shall be the gravel under foot.
I shall watch for
Slim birds swift of wing
That go where wind and ranks of thunder
Drive the wild processionals of rain.

The dust of the traveled road
Shall touch my hands and face.

Choices

They offer you many things,
    I a few.
Moonlight on the play of fountains at night
With water sparkling a drowsy monotone,
Bare-shouldered, smiling women and talk
And a cross-play of loves and adulteries
And a fear of death
              and a remembering of regrets:

All this they offer you.
I come with:
        salt and bread
        a terrible job of work
        and tireless war;
Come and have now:
        hunger
        danger
        and hate.

Graves

I dreamed one man stood against a thousand,
One man damned as a wrongheaded fool.
One year and another he walked the streets,
And a thousand shrugs and hoots
Met him in the shoulders and mouths he passed.

        He died alone
And only the undertaker came to his funeral.

Flowers grow over his grave anod in the wind,
And over the graves of the thousand, too,
The flowers grow anod in the wind.

        Flowers and the wind,
Flowers anod over the graves of the dead,
Petals of red, leaves of yellow, streaks of white,
Masses of purple sagging . . .
I love you and your great way of forgetting.

Aztec Mask

I wanted a man's face looking into the jaws and throat of life
With something proud on his face, so proud no smash of the jaws,
No gulp of the throat leaves the face in the end
With anything else than the old proud look:

> Even to the finish, dumped in the dust,
> Lost among the used-up cinders,
> This face, men would say, is a flash,
> Is laid on bones taken from the ribs of the earth,
> Ready for the hammers of changing, changing years,
> Ready for the sleeping, sleeping years of silence.
> Ready for the dust and fire and wind.

I wanted this face and I saw it today in an Aztec mask.
A cry out of storm and dark, a red yell and a purple prayer,
A beaten shape of ashes
> > waiting the sunrise or night,
> > something or nothing,
> > proud-mouthed,
> > proud-eyed gambler.

Momus

Momus is the name men give your face,
The brag of its tone, like a long low steamboat whistle
Finding a way mid mist on a shoreland,
Where gray rocks let the salt water shatter spray
  Against horizons purple, silent.

  Yes, Momus,
Men have flung your face in bronze
To gaze in gargoyle downward on a street-whirl of folk.
They were artists did this, shaped your sad mouth,
Gave you a tall forehead slanted with calm, broad wisdom;
All your lips to the corners and your cheeks to the high bones
Thrown over and through with a smile that forever wishes and
     wishes, purple, silent, fled from all the iron things of life,
     evaded like a sought bandit, gone into dreams, by God.

I wonder, Momus,
Whether shadows of the dead sit somewhere and look with deep
     laughter
On men who play in terrible earnest the old, known, solemn
     repetitions of history.
A droning monotone soft as sea laughter hovers from your kindli-
     ness of bronze,

You give me the human ease of a mountain peak, purple, silent;
Granite shoulders heaving above the earth curves,
Careless eye-witness of the spawning tides of men and women
Swarming always in a drift of millions to the dust of toil, the salt of
    tears,
And blood drops of undiminishing war.

The Answer

You have spoken the answer.
A child searches far sometimes
Into the red dust
       On a dark rose leaf
And so you have gone far
       For the answer is:
           Silence.

  In the republic
Of the winking stars
      and spent cataclysms
Sure we are it is off there the answer
    is hidden and folded over,
Sleeping in the sun, careless whether
    it is Sunday or any other day of
    the week,

Knowing silence will bring all one way
    or another.

Have we not seen
Purple of the pansy
      out of the mulch
      and mold
      crawl
      into a dusk
      of velvet?
      blur of yellow?
Almost we thought from nowhere but it was the silence,
    the future,
    working.

To a Dead Man

Over the dead line we have called to you
To come across with a word to us,
Some beaten whisper of what happens
Where you are over the dead line
Deaf to our calls and voiceless.

The flickering shadows have not answered
Nor your lips sent a signal
Whether love talks and roses grow
And the sun breaks at morning
Splattering the sea with crimson.

Under

I

I am the undertow
Washing tides of power
Battering the pillars
Under your things of high law.

II

I am a sleepless
Slowfaring eater,
Maker of rust and rot
In your bastioned fastenings,
Caissons deep.

III

I am the Law
Older than you
And your builders proud.

I am deaf
In all days
Whether you
Say "Yes" or "No."

I am the crumbler:
  To-morrow.

A Sphinx

Close-mouthed you sat five thousand years and never let out a
    whisper.
Processions came by, marchers, asking questions you answered
    with gray eyes never blinking, shut lips never talking.
Not one croak of anything you know has come from your cat
    crouch of ages.
I am one of those who know all you know and I keep my questions:
    I know the answers you hold.

Who Am I?

My head knocks against the stars.
My feet are on the hilltops.
My finger-tips are in the valleys and shores of universal life.
Down in the sounding foam of primal things I reach my hands and
    play with pebbles of destiny.
I have been to hell and back many times.
I know all about heaven, for I have talked with God.
I dabble in the blood and guts of the terrible.
I know the passionate seizure of beauty
And the marvelous rebellion of man at all signs reading "Keep Off."

My name is Truth and I am the most elusive captive in the
    universe.

Our Prayer of Thanks

For the gladness here where the sun is shining at evening on the
　　weeds at the river,
　Our prayer of thanks.

For the laughter of children who tumble barefooted and bare-
　　headed in the summer grass,
　Our prayer of thanks.

For the sunset and the stars, the women and the white arms that
　　hold us,
　Our prayer of thanks.

　God,
If you are deaf and blind, if this is all lost to you,
God, if the dead in their coffins amid the silver handles on the edge
　　of town, or the reckless dead of war days thrown unknown in
　　pits, if these dead are forever deaf and blind and lost,
　Our prayer of thanks.

　God,
The game is all your way, the secrets and the signals and the system;
　　and so for the break of the game and the first play and the last.
　Our prayer of thanks.

FOGS AND FIRES

At a Window

Give me hunger,
O you gods that sit and give
The world its orders.
Give me hunger, pain and want,
Shut me out with shame and failure
From your doors of gold and fame,
Give me your shabbiest, weariest hunger!

But leave me a little love,
A voice to speak to me in the day end,
A hand to touch me in the dark room
Breaking the long loneliness.
In the dusk of day-shapes
Blurring the sunset,
One little wandering, western star
Thrust out from the changing shores of shadow.
Let me go to the window,
Watch there the day-shapes of dusk
And wait and know the coming
Of a little love.

Under the Harvest Moon

Under the harvest moon,
When the soft silver
Drips shimmering
Over the garden nights,
Death, the gray mocker,
Comes and whispers to you
As a beautiful friend
Who remembers.

Under the summer roses
When the flagrant crimson
Lurks in the dusk
Of the wild red leaves,
Love, with little hands,
Comes and touches you
With a thousand memories,
And asks you
Beautiful, unanswerable questions.

The Great Hunt

I cannot tell you now;
    When the wind's drive and whirl
    Blow me along no longer,
    And the wind's a whisper at last—
Maybe I'll tell you then—
                        some other time.

    When the rose's flash to the sunset
    Reels to the rack and the twist,
    And the rose is a red bygone,
    When the face I love is going
    And the gate to the end shall clang,
    And it's no use to beckon or say, "So long"—
Maybe I'll tell you then—
                        some other time.

I never knew any more beautiful than you:
    I have hunted you under my thoughts,
    I have broken down under the wind
    And into the roses looking for you.
        I shall never find any
                        greater than you.

Monotone

The monotone of the rain is beautiful,
And the sudden rise and slow relapse
Of the long multitudinous rain.

The sun on the hills is beautiful,
Or a captured sunset sea-flung,
Bannered with fire and gold.

A face I know is beautiful—
With fire and gold of sky and sea,
And the peace of long warm rain.

Joy

Let a joy keep you.
Reach out your hands
And take it when it runs by,
As the Apache dancer
Clutches his woman.
I have seen them
Live long and laugh loud,
Sent on singing, singing,
Smashed to the heart
Under the ribs
With a terrible love.
Joy always,
Joy everywhere—
Let joy kill you!
Keep away from the little deaths.

Shirt

I remember once I ran after you and tagged the fluttering shirt of
    you in the wind.
Once many days ago I drank a glassful of something and the
    picture of you shivered and slid on top of the stuff.
And again it was nobody else but you I heard in the singing voice of
    a careless humming woman.
One night when I sat with chums telling stories at a bonfire
    flickering red embers, in a language its own talking to a spread
    of white stars:
            It was you that slunk laughing
            in the clumsy staggering shadows.
Broken answers of remembrance let me know you are alive with a
    peering phantom face behind a doorway somewhere in the
    city's push and fury
Or under a pack of moss and leaves waiting in silence under a twist
    of oaken arms ready as ever to run away again when I tag the
    fluttering shirt of you.

Aztec

You came from the Aztecs
With a copper on your fore-arms
Tawnier than a sunset
Saying good-by to an even river.

And I said, you remember,
Those fore-arms of yours
Were finer than bronzes
And you were glad.

            It was tears
And a path west
            and a home-going
            when I asked
Why there were scars of worn gold
Where a man's ring was fixed once

On your third finger.
                  And I call you
To come back
        before the days are longer.

Two

Memory of you is . . . a blue spear of flower.
I cannot remember the name of it.
Alongside a bold dripping poppy is fire and silk.
                       And they cover you.

Back Yard

Shine on, O moon of summer.
Shine to the leaves of grass, catalpa and oak,
All silver under your rain to-night.

An Italian boy is sending songs to you to-night from an accordion.
A Polish boy is out with his best girl; they marry next month; to-
    night they are throwing you kisses.

An old man next door is dreaming over a sheen that sits in a cherry
    tree in his back yard.

The clocks say I must go — I stay here sitting on the back porch
    drinking white thoughts you rain down.

      Shine on, O moon,
Shake out more and more silver changes.

On the Breakwater

On the breakwater in the summer dark, a man and a girl are sitting,
She across his knee and they are looking face into face
Talking to each other without words, singing rhythms in silence to
    each other.

A funnel of white ranges the blue dusk from an outgoing boat,
Playing its searchlight, puzzled, abrupt, over a streak of green,
And two on the breakwater keep their silence, she on his knee.

Mask

Fling your red scarf faster and faster, dancer.
It is summer and the sun loves a million green leaves, masses of
　　green.
Your red scarf flashes across them calling and a-calling.
The silk and flare of it is a great soprano leading a chorus
Carried along in a rouse of voices reaching for the heart of the
　　world.
Your toes are singing to meet the song of your arms:

Let the red scarf go swifter.
Summer and the sun command you.

Pearl Fog

　　Open the door now.
Go roll up the collar of your coat
To walk in the changing scarf of mist.

Tell your sins here to the pearl fog
And know for once a deepening night
Strange as the half-meanings
Alurk in a wise woman's mousey eyes.

　　Yes, tell your sins
And know how careless a pearl fog is
Of the laws you have broken.

I Sang

I sang to you and the moon
But only the moon remembers.
　　I sang

O reckless free-hearted
            free-throated rhythms,
Even the moon remembers them
  And is kind to me.

Follies

    Shaken,
The blossoms of lilac,
  And shattered,
The atoms of purple.
Green dip the leaves,
  Darker the bark,
Longer the shadows.

Sheer lines of poplar
Shimmer with masses of silver
And down in a garden old with years
And broken walls of ruin and story,
Roses rise with red rain-memories.
    May!
  In the open world
The sun comes and finds your face,
  Remembering all.

June

Paula is digging and shaping the loam of a salvia,
  Scarlet Chinese talker of summer.
Two petals of crabapple blossom blow fallen in Paula's hair,
  And fluff of white from a cottonwood.

Nocturne in a Deserted Brickyard

  Stuff of the moon
Runs on the lapping sand
Out to the longest shadows.

Under the curving willows,
And round the creep of the wave line,
Fluxions of yellow and dusk on the waters
Make a wide dreaming pansy of an old pond in the night.

Hydrangeas

Dragoons, I tell you the white hydrangeas turn rust and go soon.
Already mid September a line of brown runs over them.
One sunset after another tracks the faces, the petals.
Waiting, they look over the fence for what way they go.

Theme in Yellow

I spot the hills
With yellow balls in autumn.
I light the prairie cornfields
Orange and tawny gold clusters
And I am called pumpkins.
On the last of October
When dusk is fallen
Children join hands
And circle round me
Singing ghost songs
And love to the harvest moon;
I am a jack-o'-lantern
With terrible teeth
And the children know
I am fooling.

Between Two Hills

Between two hills
The old town stands.
The houses loom

And the roofs and trees
And the dusk and the dark,
The damp and the dew
  Are there.

The prayers are said
And the people rest
For sleep is there
And the touch of dreams
  Is over all.

Last Answers

I wrote a poem on the mist
And a woman asked me what I meant by it.
I had thought till then only of the beauty of the mist, how pearl and
     gray of it mix and reel,
And change the drab shanties with lighted lamps at evening into
     points of mystery quivering with color.

  I answered:
The whole world was mist once long ago and some day it will all go
     back to mist,
Our skulls and lungs are more water than bone and tissue
And all poets love dust and mist because all the last answers
Go running back to dust and mist.

Window

Night from a railroad car window
Is a great, dark, soft thing
Broken across with slashes of light.

Young Sea

The sea is never still.
It pounds on the shore
Restless as a young heart,
Hunting.

The sea speaks
And only the stormy hearts
Know what it says:
It is the face
        of a rough mother speaking.

The sea is young.
One storm cleans all the hoar
And loosens the age of it.
I hear it laughing, reckless.

They love the sea,
Men who ride on it
And know they will die
Under the salt of it.

Let only the young come,
    Says the sea.
Let them kiss my face
    And hear me.
I am the last word
    And I tell
Where storms and stars come from.

Bones

Sling me under the sea.
Pack me down in the salt and wet.
No farmer's plow shall touch my bones.
No Hamlet hold my jaws and speak
How jokes are gone and empty is my mouth.
Long, green-eyed scavengers shall pick my eyes,

Purple fish play hide-and-seek,
And I shall be song of thunder, crash of sea,
Down on the floors of salt and wet.
           Sling me . . . under the sea.

Pals

Take a hold now
On the silver handles here,
Six silver handles,
One for each of his old pals.

Take hold
And lift him down the stairs,
Put him on the rollers
Over the floor of the hearse.

Take him on the last haul,
To the cold straight house,
The level even house,
To the last house of all.

   The dead say nothing
   And the dead know much
   And the dead hold under their tongues
   A locked-up story.

Child

The young child, Christ, is straight and wise
And asks questions of the old men, questions
Found under running water for all children
And found under shadows thrown on still waters
By tall trees looking downward, old and gnarled.
Found to the eyes of children alone, untold,
Singing a low song in the loneliness.
And the young child, Christ, goes on asking
And the old men answer nothing and only know love
For the young child. Christ, straight and wise.

Poppies

She loves blood-red poppies for a garden to walk in.
In a loose white gown she walks
                    and a new child tugs at cords in her body.
Her head to the west at evening when the dew is creeping,
A shudder of gladness runs in her bones and torsal fiber:
She loves blood-red poppies for a garden to walk in.

Child Moon

The child's wonder
At the old moon
Comes back nightly.
She points her finger
To the far silent yellow thing
Shining through the branches
Filtering on the leaves a golden sand,
Crying with her little tongue, "See the moon!"
And in her bed fading to sleep
With babblings of the moon on her little mouth.

Margaret

Many birds and the beating of wings
Make a flinging reckless hum
In the early morning at the rocks
Above the blue pool
Where the gray shadows swim lazy.

In your blue eyes, O reckless child,
I saw today many little wild wishes,
Eager as the great morning.

SHADOWS

Poems Done on a Late Night Car

I. CHICKENS

I am The Great White Way of the city:
When you ask what is my desire, I answer:
"Girls fresh as country wild flowers,
With young faces tired of the cows and barns,
Eager in their eyes as the dawn to find my mysteries,
Slender supple girls with shapely legs,
Lure in the arch of their little shoulders
And wisdom from the prairies to cry only softly at the ashes of my
     mysteries."

II. USED UP

*Lines based on certain regrets that come with rumination upon
     the painted faces of women on North Clark Street, Chicago*

          Roses,
        Red roses,
          Crushed
In the rain and wind
Like mouths of women
Beaten by the fists of
Men using them.
   O little roses
   And broken leaves
   And petal wisps:
You that so flung your crimson
   To the sun
Only yesterday.

III.   HOME

Here is a thing my heart wishes the world had more of:
I heard it in the air of one night when I listened
To a mother singing softly to a child restless and angry in the
    darkness.

It Is Much

Women of night life amid the lights
Where the line of your full, round throats
Matches in gleam the glint of your eyes
And the ring of your heart-deep laughter:
    It is much to be warm and sure of to-morrow.

Women of night life along the shadows,
Lean at your throats and skulking the walls,
Gaunt as a bitch worn to the bone,
Under the paint of your smiling faces:
    It is much to be warm and sure of to-morrow.

Trafficker

Among the shadows where two streets cross,
A woman lurks in the dark and waits
To move on when a policeman heaves in view.
Smiling a broken smile from a face
Painted over haggard bones and desperate eyes,
All night she offers passers-by what they will
Of her beauty wasted, body faded, claims gone,
And no takers.

Harrison Street Court

I heard a woman's lips
Speaking to a companion
Say these words:

"A woman what hustles
Never keeps nothin'
For all her hustlin'.
Somebody always gets
What she goes on the street for.
If it ain't a pimp
It's a bull what gets it.
I been hustlin' now
Till I ain't much good any more.
I got nothin' to show for it.
Some man got it all,
Every night's hustlin' I ever did."

Soiled Dove

Let us be honest; the lady was not a harlot until she married a
    corporation lawyer who picked her from a Ziegfeld chorus.
Before then she never took anybody's money and paid for her silk
    stockings out of what she earned singing and dancing.
She loved one man and he loved six women and the game was
    changing her looks, calling for more and more massage
    money and high coin for the beauty doctors.
Now she drives a long, underslung motor car all by herself, reads in
    the day's papers what her husband is doing to the inter-state
    commerce commission, requires a larger corsage from year to
    year, and wonders sometimes how one man is coming along
    with six women.

Jungheimer's

In western fields of corn and northern timber lands,
    They talk about me, a saloon with a soul,
    The soft red lights, the long curving bar,
    The leather seats and dim corners,
    Tall brass spittoons, a nigger cutting ham,
And the painting of a woman half-dressed thrown reckless across a
    bed after a night of booze and riots.

Gone

Everybody loved Chick Lorimer in our town.
                Far off
            Everybody loved her.
So we all love a wild girl keeping a hold
            On a dream she wants.
Nobody knows now where Chick Lorimer went.
Nobody knows why she packed her trunk . . . a few old things
And is gone,
                Gone with her little chin
                Thrust ahead of her
                And her soft hair blowing careless
                From under a wide hat,
Dancer, singer, a laughing passionate lover.

Were there ten men or a hundred hunting Chick?
Were there five men or fifty with aching hearts?
            Everybody loved Chick Lorimer.
                Nobody knows where she's gone.

OTHER DAYS
(1900–1910)

Dreams in the Dusk

Dreams in the dusk,
Only dreams closing the day
And with the day's close going back
To the gray things, the dark things,
The far, deep things of dreamland.

Dreams, only dreams in the dusk,
Only the old remembered pictures
Of lost days when the day's loss
Wrote in tears the heart's loss.

Tears and loss and broken dreams
May find your heart at dusk.

Docks

Strolling along
By the teeming docks,
I watch the ships put out.
Black ships that heave and lunge
And move like mastodons
Arising from lethargic sleep.

The fathomed harbor
Calls them not nor dares
Them to a strain of action,
But outward, on and outward,
Sounding low-reverberating calls,
Shaggy in the half-lit distance,
They pass the pointed headland,

View the wide, far-lifting wilderness
And leap with cumulative speed
To test the challenge of the sea.

Plunging,
Doggedly onward plunging,
Into salt and mist and foam and sun.

All Day Long

All day long in fog and wind,
The waves have flung their beating crests
Against the palisades of adamant.
    My boy, he went to sea, long and long ago,
    Curls of brown were slipping underneath his cap,
    He looked at me from blue and steely eyes;
    Natty, straight and true, he stepped away,
    My boy, he went to sea.
All day long in fog and wind,
The waves have flung their beating crests
Against the palisades of adamant.

Waiting

Today I will let the old boat stand
Where the sweep of the harbor tide comes in
To the pulse of a far, deep-steady sway.
And I will rest and dream and sit on the deck
    Watching the world go by
And take my pay for many hard days gone I remember.

I will choose what clouds I like
In the great white fleets that wander the blue
As I lie on my back or loaf at the rail.
And I will listen as the veering winds kiss me and fold me
And put on my brow the touch of the world's great will.

Daybreak will hear the heart of the boat beat,
    Engine throb and piston play

In the quiver and leap at call of life.
To-morrow we move in the gaps and heights
On changing floors of unlevel seas
And no man shall stop us and no man follow
For ours is the quest of an unknown shore
And we are husky and lusty and shouting-gay.

From the Shore

A lone gray bird,
Dim-dipping, far-flying,
Alone in the shadows and grandeurs and tumults
Of night and the sea
And the stars and storms.

Out over the darkness it wavers and hovers,
Out into the gloom it swings and batters,
Out into the wind and the rain and the vast,
Out into the pit of a great black world,
Where fogs are at battle, sky-driven, sea-blown,
Love of mist and rapture of flight,
Glories of chance and hazards of death
On its eager and palpitant wings.

Out into the deep of the great dark world,
Beyond the long borders where foam and drift
Of the sundering waves are lost and gone
On the tides that plunge and rear and crumble.

Uplands in May

Wonder as of old things
Fresh and fair come back
Hangs over pasture and road.
Lush in the lowland grasses rise
And upland beckons to upland.
The great strong hills are humble.

Dream Girl

You will come one day in a waver of love,
Tender as dew, impetuous as rain,
The tan of the sun will be on your skin,
The purr of the breeze in your murmuring speech,
You will pose with a hill-flower grace.

You will come, with your slim, expressive arms,
A poise of the head no sculptor has caught
And nuances spoken with shoulder and neck,
Your face in a pass-and-repass of moods
As many as skies in delicate change
Of cloud and blue and flimmering sun.

Yet,
You may not come, O girl of a dream,
We may but pass as the world goes by
And take from a look of eyes into eyes,
A film of hope and a memoried day.

Plowboy

After the last red sunset glimmer,
Black on the line of a low hill rise,
Formed into moving shadows, I saw
A plowboy and two horses lined against the gray,
Plowing in the dusk the last furrow.
The turf had a gleam of brown,
And smell of soil was in the air,
And, cool and moist, a haze of April.

I shall remember you long,
Plowboy and horses against the sky in shadow.
I shall remember you and the picture
You made for me,
Turning the turf in the dusk
And haze of an April gloaming.

Broadway

I shall never forget you, Broadway
Your golden and calling lights.

I'll remember you long,
Tall-walled river of rush and play.

Hearts that know you hate you
And lips that have given you laughter
Have gone to their ashes of life and its roses,
Cursing the dreams that were lost
In the dust of your harsh and trampled stones.

Old Woman

The owl-car clatters along, dogged by the echo
From building and battered paving-stone;
The headlight scoffs at the mist
And fixes its yellow rays in the cold slow rain;
Against a pane I press my forehead
And drowsily look on the walls and sidewalks.

The headlight finds the way
And life is gone from the wet and the welter —
Only an old woman, bloated, disheveled and bleared.
Far-wandered waif of other days,
Huddles for sleep in a doorway,
Homeless.

Noon Hour

She sits in the dust at the walls
     And makes cigars,
Bending at the bench
With fingers wage-anxious,
Changing her sweat for the day's pay.

Now the noon hour has come,
And she leans with her bare arms
On the window-sill over the river,
Leans and feels at her throat
Cool-moving things out of the free open ways:

At her throat and eyes and nostrils
The touch and the blowing cool
Of great free ways beyond the walls.

'Boes

I waited today for a freight train to pass.
Cattle cars with steers butting their horns against the bars, went by.
And a half a dozen hoboes stood on bumpers between cars.
Well, the cattle are respectable, I thought.
Every steer has its transportation paid for by the farmer sending it to
    market.
While the hoboes are law-breakers in riding a railroad train without
    a ticket.
It reminded me of ten days I spent in the Allegheny County jail in
    Pittsburgh.
I got ten days even though I was a veteran of the Spanish-American
    war.
Cooped in the same cell with me was an old man, a bricklayer and
    a booze-fighter.
But it just happened he, too, was a veteran soldier, and he had
    fought to preserve the Union and free the niggers.
We were three in all, the other being a Lithuanian who got drunk
    on pay day at the steel works and got to fighting a policeman;
All the clothes he had was a shirt, pants and shoes — somebody got
    his hat and coat and what money he had left over when he got
    drunk.

Under a Telephone Pole

I am a copper wire slung in the air,
Slim against the sun I make not even a clear line of shadow.
Night and day I keep singing — humming and thrumming:

It is love and war and money; it is the fighting and the tears, the
    work and want,
Death and laughter of men and women passing through me,
    carrier of your speech,
In the rain and the wet dripping, in the dawn and the shine drying,
        A copper wire.

I Am the People, the Mob

I am the people — the mob — the crowd — the mass.
Do you know that all the great work of the world is done through
    me?
I am the workingman, the inventor, the maker of the world's food
    and clothes.
I am the audience that witnesses history. The Napoleons come
    from me and the Lincolns. They die. And then I send forth
    more Napoleons and Lincolns.
I am the seed ground. I am a prairie that will stand for much
    plowing. Terrible storms pass over me. I forget. The best of me
    is sucked out and wasted. I forget. Everything but Death
    comes to me and makes me work and give up what I have.
    And I forget.
Sometimes I growl, shake myself and spatter a few red drops for
    history to remember. Then — I forget.
When I, the People, learn to remember, when I, the People, use
    the lessons of yesterday and no longer forget who robbed me
    last year, who played me for a fool — then there will be no
    speaker in all the world say the name: "The People," with any
    fleck of a sneer in his voice or any far-off smile of derision.
The mob — the crowd — the mass — will arrive then.

Government

The Government — I heard about the Government and I went out
    to find it. I said I would look closely at it when I saw it.
Then I saw a policeman dragging a drunken man to the callaboose.
    It was the Government in action.
I saw a ward alderman slip into an office one morning and talk with

a judge. Later in the day the judge dismissed a case against a pickpocket who was a live ward worker for the alderman. Again I saw this was the Government, doing things.

I saw militiamen level their rifles at a crowd of workingmen who were trying to get other workingmen to stay away from a shop where there was a strike on. Government in action.

Everywhere I saw that Government is a thing made of men, that Government has blood and bones, it is many mouths whispering into many ears, sending telegrams, aiming rifles, writing orders, saying "yes" and "no."

Government dies as the men who form it die and are laid away in their graves and the new Government that comes after is human, made of heartbeats of blood, ambitions, lusts, and money running through it all, money paid and money taken, and money covered up and spoken of with hushed voices.

A Government is just as secret and mysterious and sensitive as any human sinner carrying a load of germs, traditions and corpuscles handed down from fathers and mothers away back.

Languages

There are no handles upon a language
Whereby men take hold of it
And mark it with signs for its remembrance.
It is a river, this language,
Once in a thousand years
Breaking a new course
Changing its way to the ocean.
It is mountain effluvia
Moving to valleys
And from nation to nation
Crossing borders and mixing.
Languages die like rivers.
Words wrapped round your tongue today
And broken to shape of thought
Between your teeth and lips speaking
Now and today
Shall be faded hieroglyphics

Ten thousand years from now.
Sing — and singing — remember
Your song dies and changes
And is not here to-morrow
Any more than the wind
Blowing ten thousand years ago.

Letters to Dead Imagists

EMILY DICKINSON:
You gave us the bumble bee who has a soul,
The everlasting traveler among the hollyhocks,
And how God plays around a back yard garden.

STEVIE CRANE:
War is kind and we never knew the kindness of war till you came;
Nor the black riders and clashes of spear and shield out of the sea,
Nor the mumblings and shots that rise from dreams on call.

Sheep

Thousands of sheep, soft-footed, black-nosed sheep — one by one going up the hill and over the fence — one by one four-footed pattering up and over — one by one wiggling their stub tails as they take the short jump and go over — one by one silently unless for the multitudinous drumming of their hoofs as they move on and go over — thousands and thousands of them in the gray haze of evening just after sundown — one by one slanting in a long line to pass over the hill —

I am the slow, long-legged Sleepyman and I love you sheep in Persia, California, Argentine, Australia, or Spain — you are the thoughts that help me when I, the Sleepyman, lay my hands on the eyelids of the children of the world at eight o'clock every night — you thousands and thousands of sheep in a procession of dusk making an endless multitudinous drumming on the hills with your hoofs.

The Red Son

I love your faces I saw the many years
I drank your milk and filled my mouth
With your home talk, slept in your house
And was one of you.
           But a fire burns in my heart.
Under the ribs where pulses thud
And flitting between bones of skull
Is the push, the endless mysterious command,
        Saying:
"I leave you behind—
You for the little hills and the years all alike,
You with your patient cows and old houses
Protected from the rain,
I am going away and I never come back to you;
Crags and high rough places call me,
Great places of death
Where men go empty handed
And pass over smiling
To the star-drift on the horizon rim.
My last whisper shall be alone, unknown;
I shall go to the city and fight against it,
And make it give me passwords
Of luck and love, women worth dying for,
And money.
        I go where you wist not of
        Nor I nor any man nor woman.
        I only know I go to storms
        Grappling against things wet and naked."
There is no pity of it and no blame.
None of us is in the wrong.
After all it is only this:
        You for the little hills and I go away.

The Mist

I am the mist, the impalpable mist,
Back of the thing you seek.

My arms are long,
Long as the reach of time and space.

Some toil and toil, believing,
Looking now and again on my face,
Catching a vital, olden glory.

But no one passes me,
I tangle and snare them all.
I am the cause of the Sphinx,
The voiceless, baffled, patient Sphinx.

I was at the first of things,
I will be at the last.
  I am the primal mist
  And no man passes me;
  My long impalpable arms
  Bar them all.

The Junk Man

I am glad God saw Death
And gave Death a job taking care of all who are tired of living:

When all the wheels in a clock are worn and slow and the connec-
  tions loose
And the clock goes on ticking and telling the wrong time from hour
  to hour
And people around the house joke about what a bum clock it is,
How glad the clock is when the big Junk Man drives his wagon
Up to the house and puts his arms around the clock and says:
  "You don't belong here,
  You gotta come
  Along with me,"
How glad the clock is then, when it feels the arms of the Junk Man
  close around it and carry it away.

Silver Nails

A man was crucified. He came to the city a stranger, was accused, and nailed to a cross. He lingered hanging. Laughed at the crowd. "The nails are iron," he said, "You are cheap. In my country when we crucify we use silver nails . . ." So he went jeering. They did not understand him at first. Later they talked about him in changed voices in the saloons, bowling alleys, and churches. It came over them every man is crucified only once in his life and the law of humanity dictates silver nails be used for the job. A statue was erected to him in a public square. Not having gathered his name when he was among them, they wrote him as John Silvernail on the statue.

Gypsy

I asked a gypsy pal
To imitate an old image
And speak old wisdom.
She drew in her chin,
Made her neck and head
The top piece of a Nile obelisk
    and said:
Snatch off the gag from thy mouth, child,
And be free to keep silence.
Tell no man anything for no man listens,
Yet hold thy lips ready to speak.

Alphabetical List of Titles

Alphabetical List of First Lines